FORMULA ONE

Frances Ridley

Editorial Consultant – Cliff Moon

RISING★STARS

Helping Everyone Achieve

nasen
NASEN House, 4/5 Amber Business Village, Amber Close,
Amington, Tamworth, Staffordshire B77 4RP

Rising Stars UK Ltd.
22 Grafton Street, London W1S 4EX
www.risingstars-uk.com

Every effort has been made to trace copyright holders and obtain their permission for use of copyright material. The publisher will gladly receive information enabling them to rectify any error or omission in subsequent editions.
All facts are correct at time of going to press.

Published 2006

Cover design: Button plc
Cover image: Kolvenbach/Alamy
Illustrator: Bill Greenhead
Technical artwork: IFA Design
Text design and typesetting: Nicholas Garner, Codesign
Technical adviser: Mark Rendes
Educational consultants: Cliff Moon and Lorraine Petersen
Pictures: Motoring Picture Library/NMM; pages 10, 11, 22, 28, 31, 38: Alamy; pages 5, 11, 12, 13, 16, 18, 23, 27, 29, 30, 33, 40, 41, 42, 43, 46: Getty Images; pages 7, 8, 10, 19, 24, 25, 26, 30, 31, 32, 33.

British Library Cataloguing in Publication Data.
A CIP record for this book is available from the British Library.

ISBN: 1-905056-96-6

Printed by Craft Print International Ltd, Singapore

Contents

The Formula One World Championship

The F1 World Championship has been held every year since 1950. It is run by the **FIA**.

F1 teams

There have been more than 100 F1 teams since 1950. These teams took part in the 2005 World Championship:

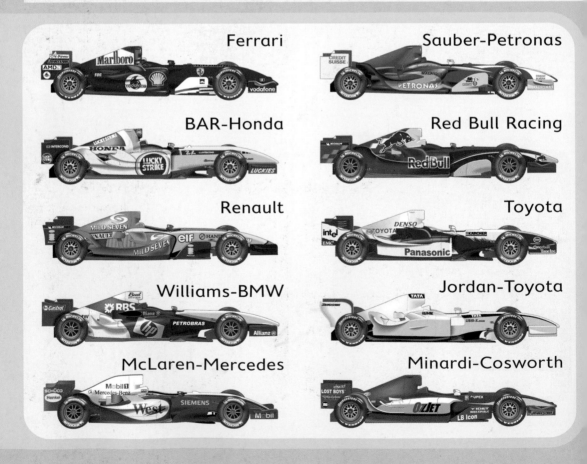

Ferrari

Sauber-Petronas

BAR-Honda

Red Bull Racing

Renault

Toyota

Williams-BMW

Jordan-Toyota

McLaren-Mercedes

Minardi-Cosworth

F1 drivers

F1 drivers need strong bodies and strong minds.

They wear helmets and **fireproof** clothes on the track.

Helmet

Fireproof gloves

Thin soles

Boots

Fireproof overalls

F1 circuits and cars

Grand Prix races are held on **circuits**.

Fast Fact!

In 2005, the EU banned F1 teams from advertising tobacco. They also banned tobacco companies from sponsoring F1 teams.

These 19 circuits were used in the 2005 World Championship.

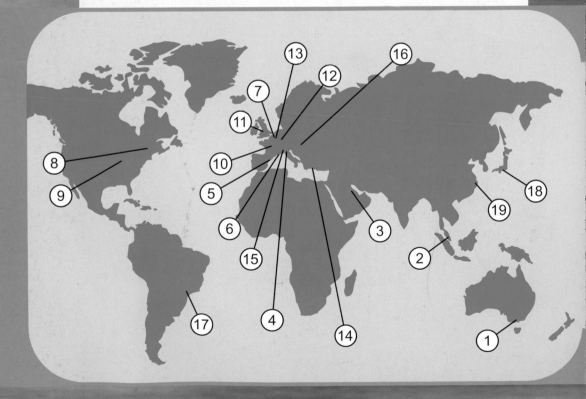

An F1 car is planned on a computer.

It is tested in a **wind tunnel** and on test tracks.

F1 cars are top secret and teams have to look out for spies.

AUSTRALIA, Melbourne

MALAYSIA, Kuala Lumpur

BAHRAIN, Sakhir

SAN MARINO, Imola

SPAIN, Catalunya

MONACO, Monte Carlo

EUROPE, Nurburgring

CANADA, Montreal

US, Indianapolis

FRANCE, Magny-Cours

⑪ BRITAIN, Silverstone

⑫ GERMANY, Hockenheim

⑬ BELGIUM, Spa Francorchamps

⑭ TURKEY, Istanbul

⑮ ITALY, Monza

⑯ HUNGARY, Budapest

⑰ BRAZIL, Sao Paulo

⑱ JAPAN, Suzuka

⑲ CHINA, Shanghai

Fangio (Part one)

Fangio was one of the best F1 drivers ever.
This is the story of his life.

Juan Manuel Fangio was born
in Argentina in 1911.

His parents were Italian and he
had five brothers and sisters.

Most racing drivers came from rich families,
but Fangio's family was very poor. He started
working in a garage when he was 12.
He learnt about engines and how to drive.

Fangio started racing when he was 18.
In 1940 he raced from Buenos Aires to Lima
and back. The race was thousands of miles
long and took two weeks.
It was hard – but Fangio won!

Fangio won many more races. He was the
Argentine Champion in 1940 and 1941.
Then the Second World War started and
Fangio had to stop racing.

Continued on page 20

A Grand Prix weekend

Thursday

The teams set up in the **paddock**.

Friday

   First practice session

   Second practice session

The teams make changes to the cars to make them go faster.

Saturday

  Third practice session

  Fourth practice session

 Qualifying session

Each driver is timed for one lap. The fastest driver will start the race from **pole position**.

 The teams talk to the **media**.

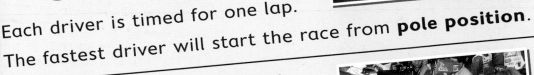

Sunday

Reconnaissance lap

 The drivers leave the pits. They do a lap and then line up on the **grid**.

Formation lap

The drivers do a lap from the grid. Then they wait for the race to start.

The race!

Five red lights come on one by one.

When all the lights go out the race begins!

Each race is around 194 miles and lasts for about 90 minutes.

Race officials use flags to give drivers warnings.

Flag	Warning
	Danger ahead — slow down and be ready to stop
	All clear
	Race has to be stopped
	Let car behind overtake
	Slippery track ahead
	Car problem — go to pit
	Go to pit (you are out of the race)
	Race is finished

Racing round Spa

Spa Francorchamps is in Belgium.

It has fast straights and tricky corners.

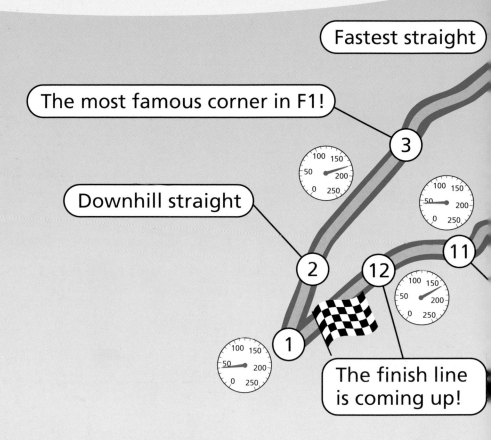

Fastest straight

The most famous corner in F1!

Downhill straight

The finish line is coming up!

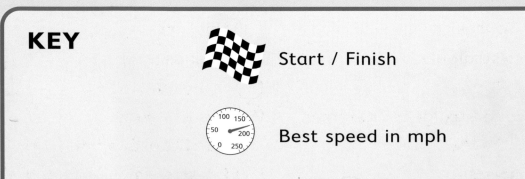

KEY

Start / Finish

Best speed in mph

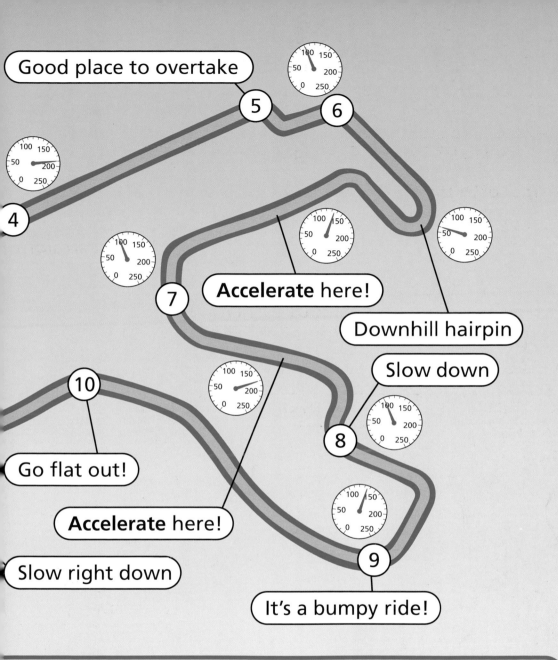

Good place to overtake

Accelerate here!

Downhill hairpin

Slow down

Go flat out!

Accelerate here!

Slow right down

It's a bumpy ride!

) La Source
) First straight
) Eau Rouge
) Second straight – Kemmell
) Les Combes
) Malmeady

(7) Pouhon
(8) Fagnes
(9) Stavelot
(10) Blanchimont
(11) Bus Stop Chicane
(12) Pit straight

Making a pit stop

Each team has its own garage called a pit.
The pits are near the Start/Finish line.
F1 cars come into the pit for fuel and tyre repairs.
A pit stop takes about seven seconds.

Each damaged tyre is changed by three mechanics.

The car is jacked up if it needs tyre changes.

The lollipop man shows the driver where to stop and when it is safe to leave.

Two mechanics fill the car with fuel.

This mechanic restarts the car if it stalls.

A mechanic stands by on each side of the car in case of fire.

One mechanic wipes the driver's visor.

The points system

The first eight cars in each Grand Prix get points.

Place	Points
1st	10
2nd	8
3rd	6
4th	5
5th	4
6th	3
7th	2
8th	1

The points are added together at the end of the season.

The driver with the most points wins the Drivers' Championship.

The team with the most points wins the Constructors' Championship.

Fernando Alonso won the 2005 Drivers' Championship with 133 points.

Alonso is a Renault driver. The other Renault driver got 58 points in 2005.

Renault won the Constructors' Championship with 191 points.

Fangio (Part two)

Fangio started racing again in 1949. He was 37, which was old for a F1 driver.
Fangio drove for Alfa Romeo in the first F1 World Championship and came second. In 1951 he won the World Championship!

In 1952, Fangio raced in the championship again. He had to drive all night to get to the Monza Grand Prix.

He got there just in time and started from the back of the grid. But he was tired and he made a mistake.

His car hit a bank and flipped over. Fangio broke his neck.

Fangio nearly died but he didn't let this beat him. He got fit again and was soon back in F1.

Continued on page 34

Ferrari

The Ferrari team was started by Enzo Ferrari in Italy.

It is the oldest team in the Championship.

Its first F1 season was in 1950 and its first car was the 125F1.

The Ferrari 125F1

Ferrari won its first Grand Prix (GP) in 1951 at Silverstone.

By 1983 it had won nine Drivers' titles and eight Constructors' titles.

The 312T

Nikki Lauda

Nikki Lauda drove the 312T in the 1975 season.

He won his first World Championship.

It was Ferrari's first title for eleven years.

The Ferrari 312T

Car Facts!

Championship points	113
Pole positions	10
GP wins	9

23

Ferrari didn't win any F1 titles from 1983 to 1999.

Then things started to get better.
In 1996 Michael Schumacher moved to Ferrari.
In 1999 Ferrari won the Constructors' title
with the F339.

The F1-2000

Rubens Barrichello, Schumacher's teammate, driving the F1-2000.

The F1-2000 was Ferrari's 47th F1 design.

Schumacher drove it in the 2000 season and won nine races!

Schumacher won the Drivers' Championship in 2000.

Ferrari won the Constructors' Championship.

Car Facts!

Championship points	171
Pole positions	10
GP wins	10

Michael Schumacher

Michael Schumacher was born in Germany in 1969.

He started kart racing **when he was four and still loves this sport!**

Schumacher's first F1 race was at Spa in 1991.

He drove for Jordan because the team's driver was in jail. Schumacher was his stand-in!

Schumacher joined Benetton in 1992. He won the World Championship in 1994 and 1995.

In 1996 Schumacher joined Ferrari.

He has won five more World Championships with Ferrari.

Driver Facts!	
World Championship titles	7
GP wins	84
Pole positions	64

Schumacher is one of the greatest F1 drivers of all time.

McLaren

The McLaren team was started in 1963 by Bruce McLaren.

Bruce Mclaren was an F1 driver. In 1968 he won the first GP for McLaren.

Sadly, he died two years later in a car crash.

The McLaren team won its first Drivers' title and Constructors' title in 1974.

James Hunt won a second Drivers' title in 1976.

He beat Nikki Lauda by one point.

McLaren had won seven more Drivers' titles by 1991.

They won the Constructors' title five more times.

The MP4/4 and MP4/13

The MP4/4 raced in 16 GPs in 1988.

It won 15 of them!

McLaren had the most powerful car and the best drivers – Ayrton Senna and Alain Prost.

MP4/4 Facts!	
Championship points	199
Pole positions	15
GP wins	15

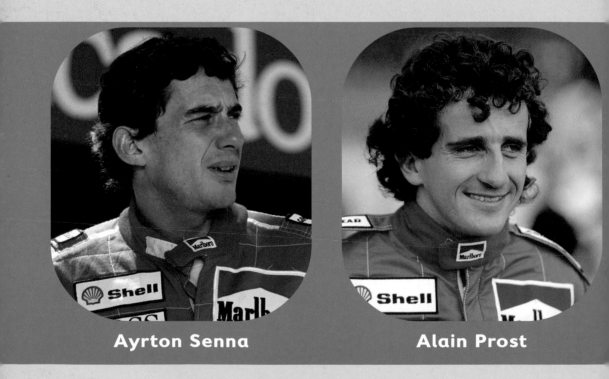

Ayrton Senna   Alain Prost

Alain Prost moved to Williams in 1992.

Ayrton Senna left McLaren in 1993 and Mika Hakkinen joined the team.

McLaren didn't win a title for the next five years.

Then, in 1998, McLaren had another great year.

Mika Hakkinen drove the MP4/13.

The McLaren MP4/13

MP4/13 Facts!	
Championship points	156
Pole positions	12
GP wins	9

Hakkinen won the Drivers' title and
McLaren won the Constructors' title.

Ayrton Senna

Ayrton Senna was born in 1960 in Brazil.

He came from a rich family, so he didn't race for money.

He raced because he loved it.

Senna drove for McLaren from 1988 to 1993.

He won three World Championships in that time.

Driver Facts!

World Championship titles	3
GP wins	41
Pole positions	65

Senna moved to Williams in 1994.

That year his car came off the track at Imola. It crashed into a wall and Senna died.

It was a great loss to F1.

Frank Williams said, "Ayrton was a greater man out of the car than in it."

Fangio (Part three)

Fangio won four more World Championships from 1954 to 1957. He drove for four different teams.

Enzo Ferrari didn't like the way Fangio swapped teams.

But Stirling Moss said it didn't matter which car Fangio drove.

Fangio was very strong. This was important as the cars were heavy and hard to handle. Drivers had to work hard to get them round the track!

Fangio's greatest race was in 1957 at Nurburgring. He was leading by 28 seconds but Maserati hadn't put much fuel in the car. This made the car lighter, but Fangio had to stop for fuel, so he lost lots of time.

Continued on the next page

At last Fangio got back on the track. There were only 12 laps to go! Fangio drove like a demon. He overtook the Ferrari driver and got into first place again. He won by 3.6 seconds!

Fangio stopped racing in 1958, but he soon had another adventure!
He was kidnapped by Cuban rebels in 1958.

The rebels let Fangio go after a day or two and he said that they had looked after him well!

Fangio died in 1995. He was 84. There is a racetrack named after him in his home town of Balcarce. There is a Fangio Museum in Balcarce, too. In 2005, the car-maker Pagani named the Zonda 2005 C12 F after Fangio.

Fangio will never be forgotten!

Renault

Renault's first F1 season was in 1977.

It raced the RS01.

The RS01

The RS01 was the first **turbocharged** F1 car.

It was a powerful car, but it had a lot of engine problems.

It was called 'The Yellow Teapot' – because it was yellow and made smoke that looked like steam!

Renault kept working on the RS01. It got better over the next two seasons.

It never won a GP but it started something new. Soon, every car on the **grid** was turbocharged.

Renault pulled out of F1 in the 1980s.

It came back in 2000.

Renault came third in the Constructors' Championship in 2004.

The R25

shark gills

The **FIA** changed the rules for cars in 2005.

Renault took a risk – it didn't make a new car.

It made changes to the R24 and came up with the R25.

The R25 was stiffer and lighter than the R24.

Renault won the Constructors' Championship.
Fernando Alonso won the Drivers' Championship.

Car Facts!

Championship points	191
Pole positions	7
GP wins	8

Fernando Alonso

Fernando Alonso was born in 1981 in Spain.

Alonso got his first kart when he was three.
It looked like a small F1 car!

When he was 18 he won the
World Junior Karting Championship.

Alonso has always wanted to win.
He says, "It is something I was born with."

In 2003 he joined Renault.

That year he became the youngest ever **pole winner** when he won the Hungarian GP.

In 2005 he became the youngest ever World Champion – at just 24 years old!

Driver Facts!

World Championship titles	1
GP wins	8
Pole positions	9

Quiz

1 How many teams were there in the 2005 World Championship?

2 How many practice sessions are there in a GP weekend?

3 What does a blue flag mean?

4 Name the most famous corner in F1.

5 What does a lollipop man do at a pit stop?

6 How many points does the sixth car get in a GP?

7 Name the oldest team in the Championship.

8 How many times has Schumacher won the Drivers' Championship?

9 What is the nickname of the RS01?

10 Alonso holds two F1 records – what are they?

Glossary of terms

accelerate	Go faster.
circuit	Track used for motor racing.
FIA	Fédération Internationale de l'Automobile.
fireproof	Will not catch fire.
grid	Starting positions for cars in a Grand Prix.
kart racing	Racing with go-karts – the karts have engines.
media	Newspapers, magazines, radio and television.
paddock	Where the F1 teams stay during a Grand Prix.
pole position	Front place on the grid.
pole winner	Car that wins from pole position.
turbocharge	Way of making an engine much more powerful.
wind tunnel	Tunnel with air rushing down it – it is like being on the race track.

More resources

Books

The Complete Book of Formula One: All Cars and Drivers since 1950, Simon Arron and Mark Hughes, Motorbooks International (ISBN: 0-76031-688-0)
This book gives you information on drivers and cars. It has 3,685 great pictures!

FIA Formula One World Championship: The Official ITV Sport Guide, Bruce Jones, Carlton Books (ISBN: 1-84222-578-9)
This book comes out each year and tells you about the circuits, the drivers, the cars and the teams.

Magazines

F1 Racing, Haymarket Magazines
The best-selling F1 magazine – news, gossip, info and great pictures.

Autosport Magazine, Haymarket Publishing
This covers all kinds of motor racing. It will keep you up to date with F1.

Websites

http://www.formula1.com/
The Official Formula One Website
Everything you need on one site: news about the latest season – and pictures; results since 1950; info on cars, teams and drivers.

http://news.bbc.co.uk/sport/hi/english/static/in_depth/motorsport/2002/formula_one/default.stm
The BBC Website – Motorsport/Formula One
Very clear introduction to F1. Check out the circuits – play the videos to go round each circuit with an F1 driver!

DVDs and Videos

50 Years of Formula One On-Board (2004) (Cat. No. 8231843)
Non-stop racing from 1950 to the present – this is the next best thing to being in the car yourself!

Secret Life of Formula One (2003) (Cat. No. LACE250)
Find out team secrets in this F1 film.

Answers

1 10

2 4

3 Let car behind overtake

4 Eau Rouge

5 Shows the driver where to stop and when it is safe to leave.

6 3

7 Ferrari

8 7

9 The Yellow Teapot

10 Youngest ever pole winner and World Champion.

Index